Risby
Sketchbook

A personal view of a Suffolk Village
by KEN VAIL

Photographs by Emily Hooton

Published by Ken Vail
Dove Cottage, The Green,
Risby, Bury St Edmunds, IP28 6QR
Tel: 01284 810626

Design, layout and drawings by Ken Vail and Sam Vail
Photographs by Emily Hooton
Technical advice & scanning by Jon Hooton and Sam Vail
Encouragement, care, and love to get me (hopefully), to the end of this project: Marian Vail.

Marian and I would like to thank both our children and express our pride in their talents and abilities which have helped to bring this project to a successful conclusion.

Printed and bound by Premier Printers, Bury St Edmunds

ISBN 978-0-9575373-0-9

Thanks to everybody at the Macmillan Unit, West Suffolk Hospital, for helping to get me through the publication of this book of drawings. Especially my Oncologist, Dr Y. Rimmer; my Oncology Nurse Specialist, Fred Tuck; Clinical Nurse Specialist in Palliative Care, Mary Macadie; my GP Registrar, Dr David Stokes; and my Practice GP at the Angel Hill Practice, Bury St Edmunds, Dr Mark Jones.

Although I am thanking the medical practice, this book is mostly about drawing and I would like to thank some of the many friends in the village who have been concerned with helping me, most significantly my dear friend June Watkins! I would also like to thank Trevor Root who has been a keen proponent of my work and insists on doing anything he can to see this project through.

It is impossible to name all the dear friends in or out of the village who have helped, but
THEY know who they are.

Below: A painting of a photograph of The Green taken c. 1901 from the collected archives of our magnificent archivist, Diana Abrey.

Introduction

I studied illustration at Cambridge School of Art in the late 1950's, under the tutelage of a marvellous artist called Paul Hogarth. I quickly realised that, although I could draw what I could see, I was never going to succeed as an illustrator. Luckily, with Paul's help, I became interested in typography and graphic design. I was soon designing bookjackets on a freelance basis whilst serving an apprenticeship in a printworks and spending two years as designer to Clive Sinclair when he was producing hi-fi equipment and starting on his first pocket calculator.

I left Sinclair in 1972 and, after eighteen months working from a back bedroom, set up offices in French's Mill, Cambridge. Apart from the occasional necessities of the job I did very little drawing for the the next 30-odd years. I concentrated on graphic design, producing about 1000 book jackets and a number of local corporate identities, including Heffers, Acorn Computers, Cambridge Cable, and Cambridge County Council, etc. The business had grown; at one point we had a staff of around a dozen, producing a range of cookery books for Sainsbury's and computer games packaging for Acorn. Following a series of market recessions, a big downturn in 1983 led to us dropping all our corporate work and specialising in the educational market, producing books for schools based on the National Curriculum.

This period coincided with me feeling the need for a new project. Nowadays, they call it a mid-life crisis, I believe! Anyway, I started researching a couple of books and one of them materialised as *Jazz Milestones* which I self-published in 1993. It was relatively successful for a jazz book, and I was approached by a publisher about the possibility of producing more, starting with a series of Jazz Diaries. My daughter, Emily, told me that she could run the business and that I should retire and concentrate on the jazz books. The business was restructured so that our children, Emily and Sam, were senior partners, and that Marian and I were junior partners. Over the next ten years I was able to write and produce another ten books.

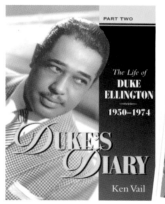  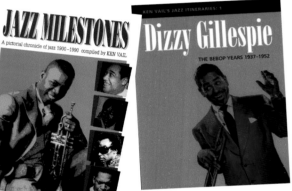

In the meantime, Marian had become increasingly disenchanted with the traffic passing by our house, and she persuaded me to move to Suffolk.

When we moved into the village in December 2005, we knew nothing about Risby, the people who lived there, or the amenities, apart from the pub where we had lunch. We had been looking for a self-contained village with a pub, a church, a community centre, maybe a convenience shop, all within a small area. Most of the Suffolk villages we had looked at seemed to be spread out over a couple of miles with a church at one end and perhaps a shop or village hall at the other. We were

lucky! The residents proved to be very friendly and accommodating and we were soon involved in village life, mostly through coffee mornings. The village was blessed by a remarkable and unique pony-tailed Australian vicar known to all as Father Pete. Shortly after we arrived in the village we were joined by Bob & Liz Henderson, who became close friends. They introduced a number of innovations, including the Friday Pub Night which morphed into the Friday Night Dinner Club at the *Crown & Castle* hosted by the landlords, June and Malcolm Missing. I had a hip replacement in December 2006 and in May 2007 was invited to be editor of *The Stile*, the Community Newsletter for the Benefice. I completely revamped the

newsletter before illness necessitated handing it over to Darren Matthews. It was the drawings I made for the covers of *The Stile* that pecipitated the idea of putting this book together, although I decided to restrict the subject matter to Risby.

Above:
Church House, and Church Cottages viewed from
the churchyard.

Below:
Risby water tower

Opposite page:
The Last Night of the Barrow
Proms.

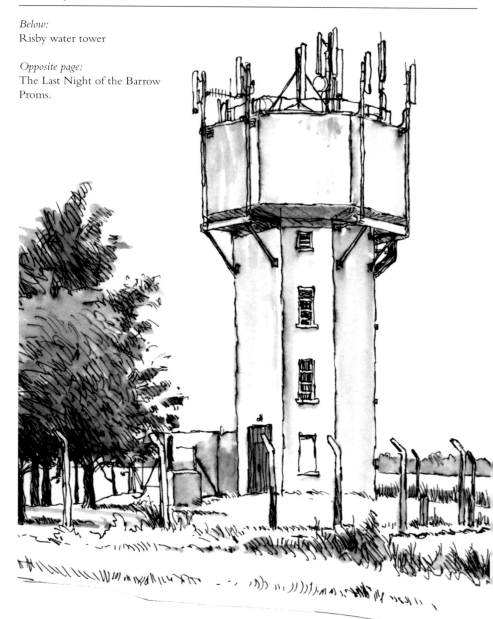

Opposite page:
Church Cottages viewed from the churchyard.

This page:
After a stormy night in August 2007, we awoke to find that a large branch had been ripped from a willow tree adjoining our property.

Opposite: A few weeks later the willow tree had been pollarded.

This page:
This is where Bob and I sat under the lych gate with a bottle of wine inspiring the formation of the art group.

Top:
Risby Village Hall

Below:
Village Hall trustees AGM.

This page:
'Southview' on Sycamore Walk.

Opposite top left:
Helen and Ken at drawing class.

Opposite top right:
Drawing club

Opposite bottom:
Church Cottages

Top left:
Elder Cottage, top of
Sycamore Walk.

Opposite page:
Hanging out the
washing on a sunny day.

Below:
Holly Cottage

Top:
War memorial

Bottom:
Sycamore Walk

Top:
School Road, Risby

Bottom:
Church House and
Church Cottage

Top:
Pub night, 'Crown & Castle'

Bottom:
External photograph of the pub.

Below:
Bob, sketching the old
water tower.

Below:
The old water tower.

Right:
Rex, sketching the old
water tower.

Top:
The Sycamores at the foot of Sycamore Walk.

Bottom:
Phil Holman at work in the bus station.

Top:
Sycamore Walk in the snow.

Bottom:
Sponsored walk round the candlestick.

Previous page:
Parish Council meetings.

This page:
Gift Horse Barbecue, above,
and morris dancers, below.

Foot of page:
Circus Ferrel on Risby Rec.

Below right:
Circus performers' accommodation.

Opposite page, top:
Pre-school on the site, under
construction.

Above:
Barrow prom with performers above and revellers below.

Above:
Lackford Lakes.

ART GROUP:

Top:
Risby Green

Opposite page bottom:
Annie Thrassell on the left and Barbara
Wilson on the right. Barbara is not a
member of the art group, but is a well loved,
respected member of the community.

Bottom left:
Brian Lillistone's talk on *'Cromwells Head'*,
Barrow History Society.

Bottom right:
New village sign.

Top left:
Queueing at Risby Village Fête.

Top right:
Diana at the Risby Village Fête.

A frightening 4 weeks of paralysis
For 4 weeks I was unable to hold a pen and was taken into
hospital. This drawing shows my first attempt.

Reg in a chair.

Adriano dos Santos at supper.

Pat Thacker at Art group.

Jane Popham at Art group.

Roger Addis at Art group.

June Watkins at Art group.

John Carter at Art group.

Lumley's Barn thatching sequence:

Right:
Becketts and Lumley's Barn.

Top left:
Bob at Art group.

Top right:
June Watkins at Art group.

Right:
Jackie at Art group.

Top:
Flempton crossroads

Left:
Macmillan Unit, West Suffolk, waiting
to see Dr Rimmer.

This page and opposite:
The Green viewed from Dove Cottage
front garden.

Right (inset):
My granddaughter, Sasha, playing
ball at the Rec.

Above:
Risby Barn's signs

Below:
Antique Barn entrance

Above:
Bob at the Village
Hall Farmer's Market.

Left:
Risby Farmer's
Market

Above:
Bus shelter in the snow.

Above:
Back garden in the snow.

Above:
Bullock's Chase Farm, Lackford Lane.

Left:
Lackford Lane, approaching village.

Opposite page top:
A view with Risby church, St Giles, in the background

Opposite page bottom:
Holly Cottage

Above:
School Road, viewed from the
corner of Hall Farm Lane, with
the pond on the left.

Right:
The Old School House

Top left:
Gage Cottage on the Flempton Road.

Top right:
Fox Cottage

Below:
Theobald House

Opposite page:
The pond at Sycamore
Walk with Little Manor
Cottage in the
background.

Above left:
The pond at Welham
Lane.

Above right:
The pond at Hall Farm
Lane.

Below right:
The Old Water Tower on
Welham Lane.

Above left:
Quiz Night at the
Crown & Castle an
opportunity to show off
your knowledge.

Above right:
The beautifully kept
Risby Apple Orchard.

Below right:
Risby Green with the
War Memorial in the
background.

Above right (opposite):
The completed
Pre-School.

Below right (opposite):
The bus shelter on the
green at South Street.

Jubilee Day, 4 June 2012:
A celebratory Barbecue held by
members of the pub's Friday
Night Dinner Club at the home
of Bev and Chris Carey.

Above:
Rodney Brook reminisces
with Steve Saunders,
while Margaret Brook
(*below right*) does the same
with Elaine Adams

Left:
Church Home

Below:
John and Kay Cornish's
house

Top left:
Stanley Woolston gives a demonstration of acrylic painting to the Art Group.

Top right:
Four new ladies from the Art Group.

Left:
June Watkins and Roger Addis, stalwarts from the beginning of the Art Group, take on board the lesson.

Above:
Woodland Close

Below right:
After Chemotherapy
and steroid therapy my
hair and beard have
disappeared, and I seem
to be storing nuts in my
cheeks. Seven weeks
later, my hair and beard
have returned, along
with my skinny face.

Above:
Risby Green

Below right:
Risby Green

Above:
Lackford Lane

Left:
Lackford lane tree

Top:
Dove Cottage, at the Cavenham-Flempton junction.

Far Left:
The War memorial and Becketts Little Manor from
Sycamore Walk.

Near Left:
The North Green looking down the footpath to the
South Green, with the Manor House on the right.

Above:
Sycamore Walk

Opposite:
Woodland Close

Main picture:
Corner of School Road

Opposite, bottom:
Walking the dog.

Above:
Hall Farm Lane

Above:
Hall Farm Cottage

Right:
North Green

Opposite, top:
Cavenham Road

Opposite, bottom left:
The Old School House

Opposite, bottom right:
Holly Cottage

Below:
From Saxham A14

Above:
Manor House

Right:
Manor House Gate

Self portrait 2012